D1524838

NFL TODAY

THE STORY OF THE
HOUSTON TEXANS

THE STORY OF THE HOUSTON TEXANS

GORDON PUESCHNER

CREATIVE EDUCATION

Cover: Running back Jonathan Wells (top),
defensive end Mario Williams (bottom)
Page 2: Linebacker DeMeco Ryans
Pages 4–5: Reliant Stadium
Pages 6–7: Texans defense, 2007

Published by Creative Education
P.O. Box 227, Mankato, Minnesota 56002
Creative Education is an imprint of
The Creative Company
www.thecreativecompany.us

Design and production by Blue Design
Design Associate: Sarah Yakawonis
Printed in the United States of America

Photographs by Corbis (Walter Bibikow/JAI),
Getty Images (Brian Bahr, Bill Baptist, Doug Benc,
Stephen Dunn, Chris Graythen, Jeff Gross, Allen
Kee/NFL, Bob Levey/NFL, Ronald Martinez, Chris
McGrath, Al Messerschmidt, Donald Miralle, Layne
Murdoch, Jerald Pinkus/NFL, Jamie Squire, Rob
Tringali/Sportschrome, Greg Trott)

Library of Congress Cataloging-in-Publication Data

Pueschner, Gordon.
The story of the Houston Texans / by Gordon
Pueschner.
p. cm. — (NFL today)
Includes index.
ISBN 978-1-58341-757-7
1. Houston Texans (Football team)—History—
Juvenile literature. I. Title. II. Series.

GV956.H68P84 2008
796.332'64097641411—dc22   2008022689

First Edition
9 8 7 6 5 4 3 2 1

CONTENTS

THE TEXANS COME TOGETHER 8

THE TEXANS STAND TALL 18

ONE STEP FORWARD, ONE BACK. 24

THE KUBIAK ERA. 30

INDEX 48

ON THE SIDELINES

BATTLE RED DAY 12

AN IMPROBABLE VICTORY 17

INSIDE THE BULL PEN 22

BACK-TO-BACK DAVIS 35

A TEXAS YOUTH MOVEMENT 41

STYLING STADIUMS 42

MEET THE TEXANS

BOB McNAIR 11

ANDRE JOHNSON 15

AARON GLENN 26

DAVID CARR 32

DeMECO RYANS 36

MARIO WILLIAMS 46

THE TEXANS COME TOGETHER

X--------------------------------

X Houston is known for its skyscrapers and involvement in both space exploration and the medical field, yet it also embraces its history, a time when horses were the only means of travel.

In 1836, real estate brokers and brothers John and Augustus Allen bought more than 6,000 acres of land on the edge of the Buffalo Bayou in eastern Texas and built a little settlement that was named Houston in honor of great Texas soldier and politician Sam Houston. It quickly became a commercial hub for the export of cotton, and by 1901, when oil was found nearby, Houston was growing at a rapid rate. In 1961, the National Aeronautics and Space Administration (NASA) moved its headquarters to Houston and helped establish it as America's fourth-largest city.

Another part of Houston's rich and colorful history involves professional football. From 1960 to 1997, fans turned out in droves to watch the Houston Oilers, who started as an American Football League (AFL) franchise before joining the National Football League (NFL). When the Oilers moved to Tennessee in 1997, fans were crushed. But in 2002, the NFL returned to Houston in the form of a new franchise. Decked out in uniforms of blue, red, and white, the club was named the Houston Texans.

On April 30, 1996, the NFL approved the Houston Oilers' move to Nashville, Tennessee, ending a streak of 37 seasons of professional football in Houston. Oilers owner Bud Adams declared that he could no longer compete financially by

playing in the aging Houston Astrodome. Houston fans were angered by the move, having supported the Oilers through thick and thin.

Houston businessman Bob McNair began working immediately to bring a new expansion team to the city. His hard work paid off in October 1999, when NFL owners voted 29–0 to award the league's 32nd franchise to Houston. The team would be placed in the American Football Conference's (AFC) South Division and would begin play in 2002.

To begin building his new team, McNair hired Charley Casserly as the team's general manager in January 2000. Casserly had spent 10 years as the general manager of the Washington Redskins. Under his watch, the Redskins won three Super Bowl titles.

Casserly's first move was to hire head coach Dom Capers. A detail-oriented coach known for his great defensive strategies, Capers had a history of success in building teams from scratch. In just two seasons, Capers had taken the expansion Carolina Panthers all the way to an appearance in the National Football Conference (NFC) Championship Game in 1996. "I know the type of work that's involved in building an expansion team," said Capers. "You have to work hard, have a plan, and not take shortcuts."

BOB McNAIR

TEAM OWNER
TEXANS SEASONS: 2002-PRESENT

In 1960, Bob McNair and his wife moved from the East Coast to Houston, Texas, where he developed a high business profile as the founder of Cogen Technologies, one of America's largest privately owned energy companies. A member of the Texas Business Hall of Fame, he was also a horseman, owning a 1,500-acre thoroughbred farm in Kentucky called Stonerside Stables. McNair got into the football business on July 3, 1997, when Houston Oilers owner Bud Adams announced that his team was officially moving to Tennessee. Many fans feared that professional football in Houston was over. And it might have been, had it not been for McNair. Immediately after the announcement, McNair laid out a plan and worked nonstop for two years, campaigning tirelessly until the league finally awarded Houston the NFL's 32nd franchise at a purchase price of a record $700 million. "It really was a feeling of importance to the city and civic pride that was the motivation for me," said McNair. "I thought it was important for the fourth-largest city in the country to have a team. I was in position, maybe the best position, to make it happen."

BATTLE RED DAY

Every season since 2003, the Houston Texans have designated one or two home games as "Battle Red Day." On these days, the players wear special red jerseys instead of their usual blue uniforms to help drum up extra support for high-profile matchups, often against division rivals. Fans, cheerleaders, the Bull Pen Pep Band, and even Toro the mascot dress in red to help get the team fired up. And the tactic seems to work. On November 2, 2003, Houston took on the powerful Carolina Panthers at Reliant Stadium dressed in Battle Red for the first time. The outlook did not appear promising for the Texans, since quarterback David Carr was out with an injury and backup quarterback Tony Banks was in his place. The game was close, but in the fourth quarter, with Houston trailing 10–7, Banks led the team down the field and finished off the drive with a 20-yard pass to tight end Billy Miller, who made a spectacular one-handed grab in the end zone to secure a 14–10 Houston win. All told, between 2003 and 2008, the Texans went 7–2 and outscored their opponents 271–142 on Battle Red Days.

The Texans began building their player roster in an expansion draft held in February 2002. Houston was able to grab several quality performers left unprotected by other NFL teams, such as five-time Pro Bowl offensive tackle Tony Boselli of the Jacksonville Jaguars, tough defensive tackles Gary Walker and Seth Payne, cornerbacks Aaron Glenn and Marcus Coleman, and linebacker Jamie Sharper. Casserly and Capers made sure to choose players who were still in their prime and showed strong leadership skills. "We know that there will be some tough times ahead," said Sharper, a starter on the Baltimore Ravens' Super Bowl championship team in 2000. "We have to be strong for the young guys."

After the expansion draft, the Texans had only a few weeks to prepare for the NFL Draft. Fortunately, the team knew exactly who it wanted to choose with the number-one overall pick: quarterback David Carr from Fresno State University. The 6-foot-3 and 230-pound passer had all the physical tools to be a great NFL quarterback—a cannon of an arm, quick feet, and great field vision. After selecting Carr, the Texans showed their commitment by signing him to a seven-year contract.

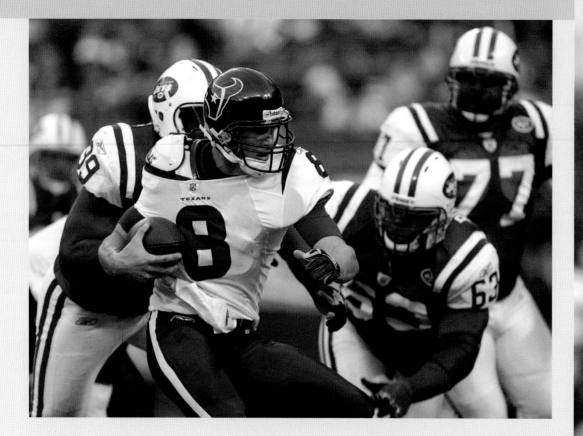

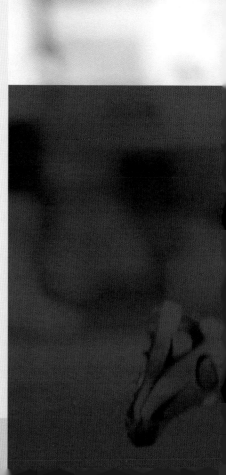

X Quarterback David Carr, Houston's first-ever pick in the NFL Draft, spent much of his rookie season on the run, trying to escape the clutches of opposing defensive linemen.

Houston also plucked some other promising offensive players from the 2002 NFL Draft. Speedy wide receiver Jabar Gaffney from Florida University gave Carr a quality passing target, while powerful linemen Chester Pitts and Fred Weary were selected to protect the young quarterback.

The Texans also found some solid players in the free-agent market, signing big-play receiver Corey Bradford from the Green Bay Packers, center Steve McKinney from the Indianapolis Colts, and linebackers Kailee Wong and Jay Foreman from the Minnesota Vikings and Buffalo Bills respectively. With the team finally assembled, it was time for the dream that was the Houston Texans to become a reality.

ANDRE JOHNSON

WIDE RECEIVER
TEXANS SEASONS: 2003-PRESENT
HEIGHT: 6-FOOT-3
WEIGHT: 222 POUNDS

It didn't take Andre Johnson long to earn a reputation as one of the NFL's elite wide receivers. At a powerfully built 6-foot-3, he could pluck balls out of the air even when he was double-covered by defensive backs, making him the kind of big-play, go-to receiver that NFL teams dream about. Johnson journeyed to Hawaii after the 2004 and 2006 seasons to play in the Pro Bowl and was the only player in the NFL in 2006 to make more than 100 catches. And he was as valuable in the community as he was on the field. Through nonprofit groups, he invited kids to attend Texans home games. He also headed the Andre Johnson Foundation, which helped raise money for local charities. In 2005, he hosted a Celebrity Weekend and raised more than $10,000. "My foundation is committed to working with kids in single-parent homes and helping them become responsible, educated citizens," Johnson said. "I grew up in a single-parent family, and I just want to help people who grew up in the same situation that I did."

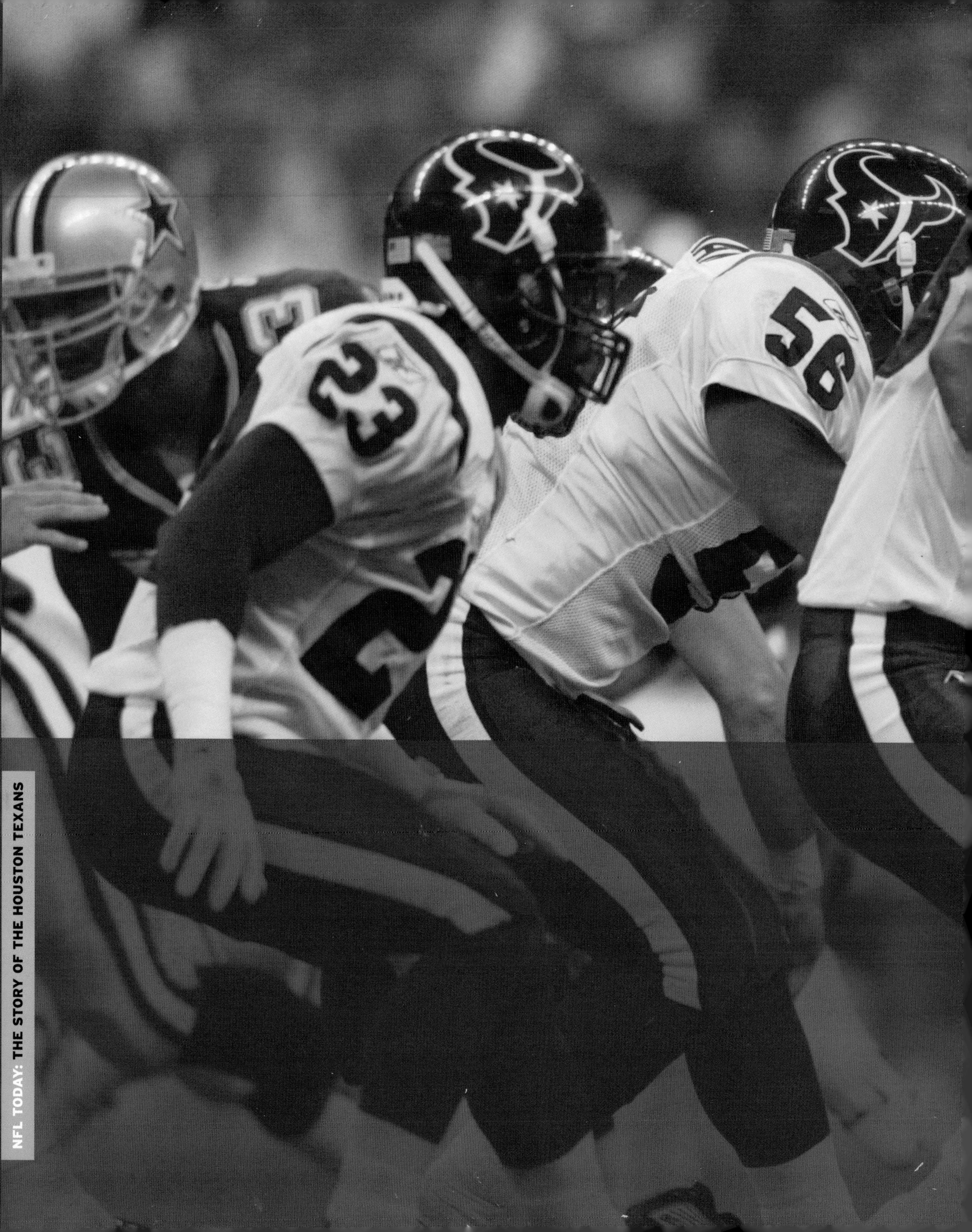

AN IMPROBABLE VICTORY

On September 8, 2002, the Texans' very first regular-season opponent was a high-profile one: the Dallas Cowboys, winners of five Super Bowls. The 69,000 fans inside Reliant Stadium didn't have to wait long for something to cheer about, as, on the third play from scrimmage, Houston quarterback David Carr zipped a 19-yard touchdown pass to tight end Billy Miller. Houston made it 10–0 on a 42-yard field goal by kicker Kris Brown before Dallas tied the game 10–10, and the momentum seemed to shift. But the Texans weren't done yet. Carr hit Corey Bradford for a 65-yard touchdown strike early in the fourth quarter, giving Houston a 17–10 lead, and the Texans defense did the rest. Tackle Seth Payne sacked Cowboys quarterback Quincy Carter in the end zone for a safety, and the Texans held on to an improbable 19–10 victory as the Houston crowd went crazy. "It was kind of unbelievable," Miller said. "We had history against us. I think just us and the coaches and probably our wives were the only ones who thought we could win."

THE TEXANS
STAND TALL

x

The Texans' first opponent in Reliant Stadium, their home field, was a familiar one to Houston fans. The five-time Super Bowl champion Dallas Cowboys—known to their fans as "America's Team"—would be the first to tangle with the Texans. For the Cowboys, the game was an opportunity to squash the young Texans and put them in their place. For the Texans, the game was a chance to make clear that Texas was not exclusively Cowboys country anymore.

The Texans jumped out to an early 10–0 lead with a 19-yard touchdown pass from Carr to tight end Billy Miller and a field goal by kicker Kris Brown. Houston's defense kept Dallas bottled up for most of the game as the Texans secured a 19–10 victory. In doing so, Houston became the first NFL expansion team since the 1961 Minnesota Vikings to win its opening game. "I don't know what the rest of the season holds," said Houston running back James Allen, "but this win will be remembered for a long, long time."

The scrappy Texans played hard throughout the 2002 season. Among the high points were Brown's late-game, 45-yard field goal to clinch Houston's first road win (a 21–19 victory over the Jacksonville Jaguars); a 16–14 win over the playoff-bound New York Giants; and a 24–6 win over the

X With the Texans' thrilling win over the Cowboys to open the 2002 season, Houston fans were able to cheer for their first hometown victory (since the days of the Oilers) in six years.

Pittsburgh Steelers that featured two long interception

returns for touchdowns by Aaron Glenn.

Houston finished its first season with a 4–12 record.

Individually, Glenn's 5 interceptions and Gary Walker's 6.5

quarterback sacks earned them each a trip to the Pro Bowl.

Carr played admirably, especially considering the young

quarterback was sacked 76 times, a new single-season NFL

record. "People wondered if David had the guts to take the

pressure of being a starter in the NFL," said Coach Capers.

"He got knocked around a lot this year, but he never flinched.

He's the real deal."

Before the 2003 season, Houston concentrated on

surrounding Carr with better blockers and more talented

receivers and runners. The team found one standout

offensive lineman on the free-agent market, signing massive

veteran tackle Zach Wiegert away from the Jaguars. Then,

in the 2003 NFL Draft, Houston selected big receiver Andre

Johnson in the first round, bruising tight end Bennie Joppru

and explosive running back Tony Hollings in the second round,

and speedy linebacker Antwan Peek in the third round. Fans

were most excited about the acquisition of the 6-foot-3 and

222-pound Johnson, who possessed a rare combination of

speed and strength. During his final season at the University

Although he notched his share of quarterback sacks, defensive tackle Gary Walker was most effective at plugging up rushing lanes.

ON THE SIDELINES

INSIDE THE BULL PEN

Located in the north end zone of Reliant Stadium is a special bleacher section called the Bull Pen. It is there that hardcore Houston fans gather to cheer on their Texans. Forty-five minutes before the game, fans led by the Bull Pen Pep Band march into the stadium, onto the field, and then into their seats. Obnoxious behavior is usually not tolerated in the rest of the stadium, but fans in the Bull Pen are encouraged to stand throughout the game and interact with opponents via such actions as turning their backs when the opposing team scores a touchdown. The Bull Pen Pep Band—a 45-member musical group that performs at all home games—is another unique element. Before games, the band can be seen marching through the parking lot among tailgaters. During the game, they play songs between quarters and when the Texans score. Between the fans and the band, Reliant Stadium can be a noisy place for opposing teams. "This place gets pretty loud when everyone's into the game," Houston receiver Andre Johnson said. "It rates up there as one of the loudest places in the NFL."

of Miami, Johnson averaged an incredible 21 yards per reception. His addition gave Carr a big target who had the potential to score every time he touched the ball.

The 2003 Texans got off to another quick start, upsetting the heavily favored Miami Dolphins 21–20 on the road in the first game and becoming the first NFL expansion team to win its first two regular-season openers. Another highlight came three weeks later in Reliant Stadium, when the Texans beat the Jaguars 24–20. The victory was sealed on the game's final play, as Carr made a one-yard touchdown dive over a pile of players. That thrilling victory had Houston fans dreaming of a winning season and a playoff berth, but the dream quickly faded when Carr and defensive standouts Gary Walker and Seth Payne were sidelined with injuries.

Although Houston finished its second season just 5–11, several players put forth impressive showings. With Hollings slowed by a knee injury, Domanick Williams—a running back from Louisiana State University picked up in the fourth round of the 2003 NFL Draft—stepped into the lineup and rushed for 1,031 yards. Johnson caught 66 passes for 976 yards in his rookie year, and veteran cornerback Marcus Coleman snared 7 interceptions. "Through good times and bad, our guys never quit this year," said a proud Coach Capers. "We took another step toward our goal of building a winner in Houston."

ONE STEP FORWARD,
ONE BACK

The Texans had proved competitive in their first two seasons, and they were determined to keep moving up the AFC South standings in 2004. Houston started the season slowly, not tasting victory until Week 3 against the Kansas City Chiefs. Down 21–14 in the fourth quarter, and facing a fourth-and-one situation, the Texans faked a punt as defensive back Jason Simmons took the snap from center and lunged forward to get the first down. Carr soon followed that up with a 37-yard pass to Johnson, who made a sensational juggling catch at the Chiefs' 8-yard line. Two plays later, Carr hit Jabar Gaffney for a touchdown to tie the game. After Houston's defense stopped the Chiefs and forced a punt, Carr again led his team down the field. With only seconds remaining, Kris Brown booted a 49-yard field goal to seal the 24–21 victory.

In the next game, running back Jonathan Wells stepped in for an injured Williams and rushed for 105 yards, helping Houston defeat the Oakland Raiders. The victory marked the first back-to-back wins in franchise history. "Our team

Willing to both give out lumps and take them, safety Marcus Coleman—a fifth-round draft pick in 1996—put together a solid, 11-year NFL career. X

AARON GLENN

CORNERBACK
TEXANS SEASONS: 2002-04
HEIGHT: 5-FOOT-9
WEIGHT: 185 POUNDS

Aaron Glenn grew up in Humble, Texas, and attended Nimitz High School, where he lettered in football, basketball, and track. The multitalented Glenn decided to pursue football and went to college at nearby Texas A&M University, where he became a two-time All-American as a defensive back and punt returner. He spent eight strong seasons as a cornerback for the New York Jets, becoming one of the NFL's best cover men, despite his short stature. In 2002, the Texans brought Glenn back to his home state by nabbing him in the league's expansion draft. And he didn't disappoint. Glenn had a career year in 2002, earning his third career trip to the Pro Bowl. His best game that season came against the Pittsburgh Steelers, when he dominated by picking off two Steelers passes and returning them for touchdowns. "He's got great quickness, great change of direction, and almost unmatched physical ability in covering people," said former Jets coach Pete Carroll. "He can score touchdowns from the defensive side of the field. He's a very special athlete."

showed what we are capable of doing," said Gary Walker. "We set a standard for the rest of the season." After seven games, Houston was a solid 4–3. For the first time in franchise history, the Texans entered the second half of the season with real hope of making the postseason.

That hope faded, however, as Houston lost five of its next eight games. Going into the last game of the season at 7–8, all the Texans had to do was overcome the struggling, 3–12 Cleveland Browns to achieve their first non-losing season. Houston marched 73 yards to score a touchdown for a 7–3 lead. But after Cleveland took back the lead, Carr had difficulty moving the Houston offense. Houston fans booed him as he threw for only 114 yards, and the Texans limped to a 22–14 defeat. "We need to be slapped in the face," said Billy Miller. "It was despicable. It was disgraceful. It was one of those learning experiences."

Despite the crushing loss, Houston had posted its best season to date, going 7–9. Johnson set a team record with 1,142 receiving yards and became the first Texans offensive player to earn a trip to the Pro Bowl. Williams also had a season to remember, carrying the ball for 13 touchdowns.

Unfortunately, after their step forward in 2004, the Texans took a step back in 2005. In their season opener

against the Buffalo Bills, the Texans were hoping for the same magic they had captured in years past on opening day. After falling behind 12–0, the Texans finally scored on a quarterback sneak on fourth-and-goal in the third quarter, narrowing the score to 12–7. But Houston could not muster another score and fell 22–7. That was only the beginning of the rough times, as the Texans dropped their next five games for a 0–6 start.

Houston finally notched a victory in Week 8, when its offense came alive against the Browns. Carr threw some long bombs and connected with rookie wide receiver Jerome Mathis for a 34-yard touchdown strike. Mathis also added a 63-yard kick return late in the fourth quarter that set up the game-winning field goal. The fast-rising rookie continued to shine for the rest of the season, gaining 1,542 total yards in kick returns—and scoring 2 return touchdowns—and making the Pro Bowl. Despite his heroics, the Texans won only one more game and ended the season with a franchise-worst 2–14 record. "I think that we've underachieved this season," McNair said glumly. "I think that everyone expected us to do more."

X The career of halfback Domanick Williams was brilliant but brief; he rushed for more than 1,000 yards in 2003 and 2004, but a knee injury forced his retirement after 2005.

THE KUBIAK ERA

X --

To shake up the struggling franchise, McNair fired coach Dom Capers two days after the 2005 season ended. During his four seasons in Houston, Capers had built a combined record of just 18–46. "I understand the job as the head football coach is to win games," Capers said. "But when you put your heart and soul into something and it doesn't work the way you want it or anticipate it to, it's disappointing."

To replace Capers, the Texans hired former Denver Broncos offensive coordinator Gary Kubiak as the second head coach in team history. In his 11 years as a coordinator, Kubiak had helped guide the Broncos to back-to-back Super Bowls and three AFC West Division titles, and he had sent 28 different offensive players to the Pro Bowl. "The number-one thing you need to do to get things going is to have aspirations and to have a standard," said Kubiak. "My dream is to see this city win a championship someday."

In the 2006 NFL Draft, Coach Kubiak and the Texans picked up smart linebacker DeMeco Ryans in the second round and tight end Owen Daniels in the fourth. But the Texans' most promising—and controversial—draft choice was the first overall pick, defensive end Mario Williams out of North Carolina State University.

X Gary Kubiak had an unremarkable career as an NFL quarterback— backing up Broncos great John Elway—but earned acclaim as an assistant coach for the 49ers and Broncos.

MEET THE TEXANS

DAVID CARR

QUARTERBACK
TEXANS SEASONS: 2002-06
HEIGHT: 6-FOOT-3
WEIGHT: 216 POUNDS

David Carr was supposed to be the face of the Houston franchise. In 2002, he was the first overall pick in the NFL Draft and the Texans' first-ever draft choice. As a college senior, Carr had been a finalist for the Heisman Trophy (as college football's best player), and scouts raved over his accurate passes, his ability to read defenses, and his great work ethic. "He has the best of both worlds—a young kid with talent, the young gun with bravado, but also with maturity, the calmness, the stability," said former Tampa Bay Buccaneers quarterback Trent Dilfer. Carr showed those qualities in his first professional game, leading the new franchise to a memorable victory over the Cowboys. But in the seasons that followed, the Texans struggled to give Carr NFL-caliber pass protection, and as he was frequently sacked, his confidence and skills seemed to decline. Even though the young quarterback completed an impressive 60 percent of his passes throughout his Houston career, he never led Houston to a winning record. After the 2006 season, the Texans released him.

The 2006 Draft featured some exceptional college players, including fast and flashy running back Reggie Bush and big quarterback Vince Young, a Houston native who had just led the University of Texas to a national championship. Fans and football experts across the country assumed Houston would select one of the two offensive stars. So when Kubiak and general manager Charley Casserly announced that Houston had instead signed Williams to a 6-year, $54-million contract, it put the sports world in a tizzy. Most of the Texans fans who were at Reliant Stadium for a public draft party booed the

X Defensive end Mario Williams's rare combination of size, speed, and intensity made him the number-one pick in the 2006 NFL Draft.

choice. "It's a decision that took us a lot of time to make," said Casserly, "but at the end of the day, we felt this was the best player for our football team."

On September 10, 2006, Kubiak led the Texans against the Philadelphia Eagles in his coaching debut. The game started well, as the Texans drove down the field on their first possession and scored a touchdown, but they ultimately came up short, 24–10. Houston lost the next two games before Kubiak claimed his first coaching victory in Week 4, with the Texans beating the Dolphins 17–15.

Over the next eight games, Houston went 3–5, beating the divisional rival Jaguars twice. But in Week 14 against the Tennessee Titans, Carr passed for only 140 yards as the Texans lost 26–20 in overtime. The next game, Carr turned in another poor performance, throwing four interceptions in a 40–7 loss to the New England Patriots. Fans began booing Carr, but Kubiak knew that the whole team needed improvement. "The quarterback gets a lot of the credit and he gets a lot of the blame, but as a football team, we have to look in the mirror, because there are plenty of mistakes in a lot of areas," the coach said.

The Texans rebounded to win their final two games of the season, one of them against the Colts. Veteran running

BACK-TO-BACK DAVIS

On December 30, 2007, the Houston Texans went into their final game of the season with a 7–8 record. Only 60 minutes and their division rivals, the Jacksonville Jaguars, stood in the way of Houston's first .500 season. In the second quarter, with the scored tied 14–14 and only 15 seconds remaining before halftime, fleet-footed Houston receiver Andre Davis fielded a kickoff and sprinted across 97 yards of turf for a touchdown to give the Texans the lead. "I think I have that type of sneaky speed where a lot of guys don't think I'm going to run that fast until I get by them," explained Davis. On the opening kickoff of the second half, Houston received the ball again … and again Davis zigzagged his way to a touchdown, this time going 104 yards. As Davis coasted into the end zone the second time, he became just the seventh player in NFL history to record touchdowns on back-to-back kick returns. Behind Davis's heroics, the Texans won 42–28 and secured a franchise-best 8–8 record.

DeMECO RYANS

LINEBACKER
TEXANS SEASONS: 2006–PRESENT
HEIGHT: 6-FOOT-1
WEIGHT: 239 POUNDS

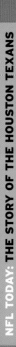

When DeMeco Ryans came out of the University of Alabama and entered the 2006 NFL Draft at "only" 6-foot-1 and 239 pounds, many scouts thought he was too small to become a star middle linebacker. But instead of seeing his supposed physical limitations, the Texans saw his playmaking ability, great instincts, and upbeat attitude. "He's got some special leadership qualities about him," said linebackers coach Johnny Holland. "He's got the [ability to get] people around him to play better." From day one, the easygoing Ryans proved that he was up to the challenge of leading an NFL defense. With a rarely seen combination of determination, confidence, and intelligence, he led the league with 126 solo tackles and earned the NFL Defensive Rookie of the Year award. In one game against the Oakland Raiders, he forced one fumble, recovered another, sacked the quarterback, and intercepted a pass, becoming the first player in Texans history to do all four in one game. "He's been exceptional," Houston head coach Gary Kubiak said. "I think we can build our football team around him."

back Ron Dayne, a new addition, rushed for 153 yards and 2 touchdowns, and Kris Brown kicked a last-second, 48-yard field goal to help Houston defeat the high-powered Colts for the first time in 10 tries. Rookie running back Chris Taylor then stepped up with 99 rushing yards and a touchdown in Houston's final win of the season, against the Browns.

At the conclusion of the 6–10 season, the team took a hard look at Carr, who seemed to be regressing, having thrown 23 interceptions and led Houston to only 8 victories over the previous 2 seasons. In March 2007, the Texans made a major change by releasing Carr and trading with the Atlanta Falcons for 25-year-old quarterback Matt Schaub, who had backed up star Michael Vick the previous three seasons. "We

X Thanks to the efforts of such players as rookie halfback Chris Taylor, the 2006 Texans outran opponents for wins in their last two games.

wanted a player who's ready to go into his prime, and that's what this young man is," Kubiak said. "This guy is ready for his opportunity to run a football team." Before the start of 2007, the Texans also signed former Green Bay Packers star running back Ahman Green and drafted defensive lineman Amobi Okoye.

In the first game of the 2007 season, the Texans whipped the Kansas City Chiefs 20–3. Mario Williams had the best game of his career, making two sacks and returning a Chiefs fumble for a Texans touchdown. Offensively, Schaub and Johnson hooked up for a 77-yard touchdown pass. The next week, Houston defeated the Carolina Panthers 34–21 on the road, overcoming an early 14-point deficit. For the first time in team history, Houston was 2–0.

The Texans struggled the next few weeks, though, losing three of the following four games. In Week 7 against the Titans, Houston found itself in a 32–7 hole after three quarters. But backup quarterback Sage Rosenfels, playing in place of an injured Schaub, didn't let his team quit. He rallied the Texans in the fourth quarter, throwing 4 touchdown passes, including a 53-yard strike to Andre Davis. Although the incredible comeback fell just short, with the Texans losing 38–36, the team inspired its fans with its never-say-die attitude. Even with injuries sidelining key players such as Johnson, Green, and Schaub, Houston continued to battle, finishing the season 8–8. "It's huge," defensive end N. D. Kalu said. "You've got to start somewhere, and this is just another stepping stone. We won 6 last year and 8 this year, and hopefully we'll win 11 next year."

Despite Kalu's optimism, the Texans' 2008 season could hardly have started worse. First, Reliant Stadium was damaged by Hurricane Ike in September. Then, Houston began the season by losing its first four games. The most painful loss occurred in the fourth game—the franchise's 100th overall—versus the Colts. The Texans led their rivals 27–10 with about four minutes left in the game before everything fell apart. As Rosenfels coughed up 2 costly fumbles, the Colts scored 21 points within barely 2 minutes to win 31–27.

Remarkably, the Texans bounced back from that devastating loss by assembling the first three-game winning streak in club history. Several rising stars helped make the turnaround possible. Rookie halfback Steve Slaton exploded onto the NFL scene by dashing for more than 1,000 yards. Wideout Kevin Walter paired with Johnson to give Houston a dynamic one-two receiving combination, while young

A TEXAS YOUTH MOVEMENT

At the start of the 2007 season, the Houston Texans featured one of the youngest defenses in the NFL, with more than 20 players under the age of 30. On most teams, such excessive youth might have been a problem, as it generally takes time for NFL newcomers to learn new formations and techniques before they can excel. But Houston had a core of talented youngsters who played with a maturity beyond their years. Twenty-three-year-old linebacker DeMeco Ryans won NFL Rookie of the Year honors in 2007, and 22-year-old end Mario Williams (pictured, left) posted 14 sacks to emerge as a star. An even younger standout was 20-year-old tackle Amobi Okoye (pictured, right), who had been 19 when he was drafted in April 2007. The 6-foot-2 and 300-pound Okoye blasted through opposing offensive lines to notch 5.5 sacks, while fellow rookie Fred Bennett, a cornerback, made his own contributions with 3 interceptions. "We've got a lot of young talent on the defense and on the team as a whole," said 25-year-old defensive tackle Travis Johnson. "We're just excited for each other."

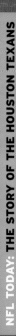
ON THE SIDELINES

STYLING STADIUMS

Houston has a rich history as a trendsetter in stadium technology. In 1965, the city introduced the Astrodome, the world's first domed stadium, as a home for both football's Houston Oilers and baseball's Houston Astros. In 2002, Houston built Reliant Stadium at a cost of $352 million. Reliant Stadium was the first NFL arena to have a retractable roof; the roof was made of translucent, Teflon-coated fiberglass and could open and close in just 10 minutes. Reliant Stadium housed two 360-foot-wide scoreboards, one above each end zone. The stadium also featured a 10,000-square-foot weight room (the largest in the league) that included a three-lane pool. In addition to its state-of-the-art features, Reliant quickly became known as a tough place to play, as cheering fans sat closer than usual to the edge of the field, making it difficult for opposing teams to hear. Houston players such as safety Eric Brown appreciated both the stadium's lush playing surface and its home-crowd volume. "The grass is easy on your body," he said, "and the fans are right on top of you."

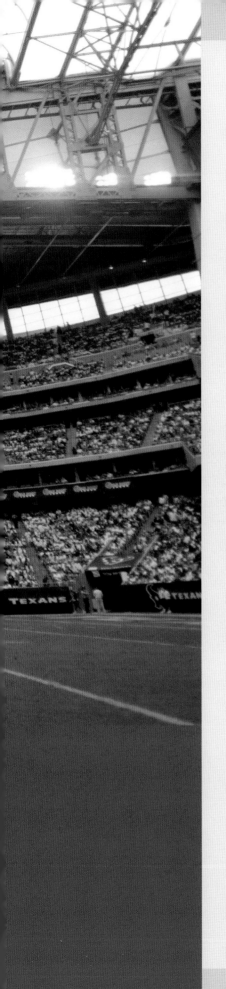

cornerback Jacques Reeves put up big numbers of both

tackles and interceptions.

After their down-and-up seven-game start, the Texans

proceeded to lose another three straight games, then win

four in a row. Among the most satisfying of those late-season

wins was a 24–21 road victory over the Green Bay Packers in

which Houston set a team record with 529 offensive yards.

Although the Texans ultimately fell short of the playoffs, the

X Bruising running back Ron Dayne was part of Houston's "platoon" rushing attack, wearing a Texans uniform in 2006 and 2007.

X Although Houston featured one of the NFL's lowest-ranked defenses in 2008, the young Texans showed signs of reversing that trend.

MARIO WILLIAMS

DEFENSIVE END
TEXANS SEASONS: 2006-PRESENT
HEIGHT: 6-FOOT-7
WEIGHT: 291 POUNDS

When Mario Williams was selected with the top overall pick in the 2006 NFL Draft, some Houston fans booed, and others cried. After all, NFL experts had been saying for months that the struggling franchise had lucked out in the draft by getting their choice of one of two surefire stars—fleet-footed running back Reggie Bush or 6-foot-5 quarterback Vince Young—and now Houston had passed on both. But those fans simply had not seen in Williams what the Texans' scouts had. The defensive end from North Carolina State was huge, fast, and agile, and he had a knack for bursting through opposing lines for game-altering sacks. "He can change a game the way he rushes the passer and the problems he presents for an offensive team," said Texans coach Gary Kubiak. In 2006, Williams fought through a foot injury to start all 16 games—a show of determination that earned him the respect of his teammates. Then, in 2007, as Bush struggled in New Orleans and Young endured his own ups and downs in Tennessee, Williams silenced any remaining critics by notching 14 sacks and 59 tackles to emerge as a bona fide star.

excitement level in Houston was rising. "We're getting used to winning around here, and that's what we've been looking for," said Ryans.

In just a few short years, Houston football fans have cast off memories of the departed Oilers and embraced a new team just beginning the difficult quest of capturing an NFL title. That road may be long, but with a roster bearing such names as Williams, Ryans, and Schaub, the Texans faithful continue to cheer with the confidence that championship flags will soon be flying over Texas.

With an improving offense and the support of their passionate fan base, the Texans hoped to soon capture their first AFC South title. **X**

INDEX

Allen, James 19

Banks, Tony 12

Battle Red Days 12

Bennett, Fred 41

Boselli, Tony 13

Bradford, Corey 14, 17

Brown, Eric 42

Brown, Kris 17, 19, 24, 37

Bull Pen 22

Bull Pen Pep Band 12, 22

Capers, Dom 10, 13, 20, 23, 31

Carr, David 12, 13, 14, 17, 19, 20, 23, 24, 27, 28, 32, 34, 37

Casserly, Charley 10, 13, 33, 34

Coleman, Marcus 13, 23

Daniels, Owen 31

Davis, Andre 35, 39

Dayne, Ron 37

first season 17, 19–20

Foreman, Jay 14

Gaffney, Jabar 14, 24

Glenn, Aaron 13, 20, 26

Green, Ahman 39, 40

Hollings, Tony 20, 23

Houston Oilers 9–10, 11, 42, 47

Johnson, Andre 15, 20, 22, 23, 24, 27, 39, 40

Johnson, Travis 41

Joppru, Bennie 20

Kalu, N. D. 40

Kubiak, Gary 31, 33, 34, 36, 39, 46

Mathis, Jerome 28

McKinney, Steve 14

McNair, Bob 10, 11, 28, 31

Miller, Billy 12, 17, 19, 27

NFL records 20, 23

Okoye, Amobi 39, 41

Payne, Seth 13, 17, 23

Peek, Antwan 20

Pitts, Chester 14

Pro Bowl 13, 15, 20, 26, 27, 28

Reeves, Jacques 43

Reliant Stadium 12, 17, 19, 22, 23, 33, 40, 42

Rookie of the Year award 36, 41

Rosenfels, Sage 39, 40

Ryans, DeMeco 31, 36, 41, 47

Schaub, Matt 37, 39, 40, 47

Sharper, Jamie 13

Simmons, Jason 24

Slaton, Steve 40

Taylor, Chris 37

team records 27, 28, 35, 40, 43

Walker, Gary 13, 20, 23, 27

Walter, Kevin 40

Weary, Fred 14

Wells, Jonathan 24

Wiegert, Zach 20

Williams, Domanick 23, 24, 27

Williams, Mario 31, 33–34, 39, 41, 46, 47

Wong, Kailee 14